HOW DYSLEXICS WILL RULE THE FUTURE

Tristan Sunday

ALSO BY TIFFANY SUNDAY

Dyslexia's Competitive Edge
You Posted What!?

How Dyslexics Will Rule the Future

Artificial Intelligence and Automation
Are Disrupting Our Economy
Creating an Employment Demand for
Creative, Innovative, Problem-Solvers

Tiffany Sunday

Tilton House Press
Dallas, Texas

Published by Tilton House Press

ISBN: 978-0-578-40159-1

LIBRARY OF CONGRESS CATALOGING-IN-PUBLICATION DATA

Sunday, Tiffany
How Dyslexics Will Rule the Future

ISBN-13: 978-0-578-40159-1

For Brandon, my son

For Shepherd, our loyal and patient
German Shepherd who slept while I typed.

Contents

Write your creative thoughts here:

Introduction

"Imagination is more important than knowledge."
–Albert Einstein

We crave to know why, search for things, explore the unknown, envision possibilities yet to be created, with an unbreakable drive that knows no bounds. Dyslexia is invisible. We, dyslexics think and process information differently which makes it difficult for individuals to understand our thought processes.

This difference, which at times is displayed with quirky social behaviors, word retrieval failures, and misspellings often hides the dyslexic brain's untapped endless supply of creativity and innovation. For the past six years, I have been researching and studying how advanced technologies will disrupt and transform talent acquisition, employment, the definition of work, and ultimately our economy and social structure.

My research uncovered emerging trends that indicate a growing demand for human creativity and innovation along with evidence that humanity, as we know it, is undergoing a paragon transformation as we enter the Fourth Industrial Revolution.

Progress requires disruptive thinking. Often, we fall into a rut and continue with our everyday routines and habits without questioning "Why" or asking important questions such as, "Are we missing something?" or "Are we going down the wrong path?" I asked these questions over and over while reviewing information and conducting interviews.

I imagined how these technologies would redesign and redefine our definition of work. I thought about how tasks could be completed using virtual reality workstations. I wondered about the potential jobs that would be available for my son when he graduates from college. I imagined our conversations as he describes his first job.

For a moment, let's visit 2025. "Work is good mom. I use verbal and visual commands to complete my work tasks. I am designing a new visual workstation today. I'll send you a link so you can see what I created." I wondered while using these advanced technologies would he forget that he is dyslexic?

Would it be possible that in the very near future, artificial intelligence (AI) and virtual reality (VR) would eliminate many of the challenges we face in a text-based work environment? Impossible? Not really. Think about how often we auto dictate text messages and emails. Think about the voice commands we give Chrome, Siri, Alexa, and Echo.

My son says I talk too much to my Mac. While I am on the computer, I ask Siri or Chrome how to spell words or provide the weather forecast. About once a month, I test Siri's programming capabilities. Maybe someday, I can train Siri to mitigate my dyslexia.

From my research, four emerging trends were observed that have the potential to provide employment opportunities previously unavailable to dyslexics and neurodiverse individuals. These trends also highlight the importance of human creativity.

As one neuroscientist mentioned at the 2017 International Dyslexia Conference in Atlanta, Georgia, "the world has finally caught up to dyslexics and individuals who think differently." To pursue these new opportunities, enterprises, and organizations will need to understand the impact of AI and automation on employment and how the digital disruption is the catalyst for these emerging trends, while at the same time envisioning future jobs. Before we can discuss these jobs and provide dyslexics with a revised career roadmap, the perception of dyslexia and neurodiversity in the workplace must change.

As these trends, driven by advanced technologies, become woven into our economy, one industry at a time, to remain competitive,

13

hiring neurodiverse employees and workers will be a necessity.

Emerging Trends

- Instead of relying solely on a text-based aptitude we are transitioning to a visual-based intellect or a combination of both.

- The use of digital communication and social media graphics as a new language will redefine literacy and communication transforming our work environments.

- The accelerated use of talent management system platforms intergraded with deep learning will further separate talent into defined cognitive groups, disrupt employment, and change our definition of work.

- A group of global enterprises is creating talent programs designed to hire neurodiverse professionals for their strengths and talents.

The employment benefit and economic value seen in these trends can only be achieved when talent matching systems include a multi-diverse talent pool. Companies and organizations need to be mindful of the unconscious coding bias, especially when seeking creative outliers to gain a competitive edge. The majority of these systems are designed to locate high achievers.

Within the education and dyslexia community, we must reduce the amount of time spent talking about the associated weaknesses and how dyslexics need *to be fixed* and redirect our energy towards supporting our abilities, skills, and strengths through innovative educational instruction and assistive technology.

The purpose of this book is to discuss the impact of advanced technologies, how employment is transforming, and how employees with dyslexia can provide a competitive advantage. Most importantly, this book's overarching goal is to emphasize the need for human creativity. I divided this book into three sections.

The first four chapters discuss advanced technologies, the redefining of literacy, and the future of work. The middle section covers future employment projections and current career opportunities created by AI, automation, and reality technologies. The final section discusses workplace strategies, the unspoken side of dyslexia, and lifestyle insights.

For this book, I used dyslexics and neurodiverse in broad terms. Each person is different. Our strengths and weaknesses vary. My son and are both dyslexic. We share common traits, and then there are areas where our strengths differ. A secondary purpose of this book is to discuss how advanced technologies will create new work opportunities and to change the perception of dyslexia in the workplace.

Technology does not create the future, we do. Enterprises and organizations need visionaries, individuals who can realistically imagine the future to build a sustainable working environment and global economy. Individuals who can realistically envision the future. Who, in their mind's eye, can craft a vision that is realistic, tangible, and concrete. A concept that excites individuals and combines the best of the human spirit, ingenuity, and technology.

We are at a digital stop sign in the history of humanity. The decisions we make today will determine how we create our future. Within the next five years, AI and automation will define and measure every aspect of our work environment and personal lifestyles. The tiny edge against these highly sophisticated machines is human-generated ingenuity and diversity.

On the surface, AI gives the illusion of increasing our innovation. However, I believe advanced AI and innovation have an inverse relationship. Original ideas, different worldviews, and strategic complex problem-solving can only be generated from the human brain.

Write your creative thoughts here:

Chapter One

Artificial Intelligence, Automation, and Advanced Technologies

"Rapid change is not limited to technology, but encompasses society and demographics as well."
—Deloitte Consulting,
Global Human Capital Trends Report 2017

Artificial Intelligence is a popular topic. Dozens of articles and blogs appear weekly discussing the disruptions, advantages, and the number of jobs that will need to be retooled because of AI. This book focuses on four technologies: AI, automation, augmented and virtual reality. Included in this chapter is a brief mention of quantum computing as it is the next technology that has the potential to transform humanity and our economy significantly.

How we define and use these technologies and software applications continues to change. Often, we fail to recognize how we modify our behaviors to adapt to these technologies. John Brandon, a contributing editor for *Inc. Magazine,* wrote about several studies conducted to determine how many times we check our mobile devices. For most of us, it's in the thousands of times a day, which equates to hundreds of minutes of lost time and productivity. Subconsciously, we are adapting our human behaviors when we interact with these technologies, which creates a ripple effect causing a cultural and economic value shift.

Remembering the human component when discussing these advanced technologies is crucial. Not only is AI and automation disrupting and transforming employment, work and our global economy, these systems are also changing how we interact with technology and each other. For continuity, I defined these technologies as interpreted in this book.

Artificial Intelligence (AI)

The definition of AI and machine learning is evolving. Bernard Marr's article for *Forbes.com*, "The Key Definitions of Artificial Intelligence That Explain Its Importance", provides historical background for the definition and then explain how AI is used today as a model for reasoning.

There are two aspects of AI: machine learning and deep learning. Machines are programmed to develop a cognitive problem-solving aptitude with the ability to learn from itself and then recognize patterns within the labeled data the system consumes. Labeled data is unlabeled data that has been categorized by the program as a means to organizes data points. Assigning labels is similar to when kindergarten students learn how to read, taking unknown letters and sounds and creating a link between the two.

AI uses every computing capability available to reduce complex information into simplified bits of data to make an informed decision. AI learns from trial and error to solve complex problems and make seamless decisions with the goal of simplifying the process by using the most optimized and efficient means available. In other words, AI is designed to think and reason like humans.

Deep learning is a subset of AI where machines learn independently from unlabeled or unidentified data. Deep learning is when these advanced platforms learn and discover something new without any help from humans. It's like when your teen is surfing YouTube and learns how to start a business. It is passive learning with significant potential to find beneficial and transformative information.

Automation

Automation occurs when the process can be completed with little to no human interaction. Think mass marketing emails, out of the office responses, tasks that are performed over and over without human oversight. When we combine the power of artificial intelligence and deep learning with automation, we can, in the future create a Siri who can solve advanced problems from managing business functions such as operations and accounting to anticipating our personal needs.

Processing new loans to accepting college applications, automated systems are interwoven within every aspect of our world. AI will continue to evolve while gaining increased cognitive capability with each iteration. Automated systems are intergraded in all professions and at all levels of employment from retail employees to senior partners. AI by itself is driving significant disruption. When AI is combined with automation, the impact is exponential.

Augmented Reality and Virtual Reality

Augmented Reality (AR) is when images are overlaid onto an object. One of the most familiar AR applications is the superimposed yellow line across the football field during televised games. AR software applications are used in multiple

22

settings, such as helping women apply makeup to navigating through busy international airports or determining if the IKEA furniture you selected will fit in your home.

Virtual Reality (VR) is using a real environment with images projected onto a surface, picture, or person. VR is different from augmented reality, as the technology requires a pair of goggles or a VR helmet that is used with the software application. When wearing VR goggles, the software produces an artificial environment complete with sights and sounds. Your actions can partially be included within the environment. If you have yet to experience VR, I recommend testing the technology at a retailer or event. Two years ago, while attending Dallas Startup Week, I tested the Sony VR headset. The best way to understand AR and VR is to experience these technologies.

Recent software upgrades and design improvements are enabling companies and schools to use VR as an on-the-job training device or enabling high school students to visit out-of-state colleges virtually.

This summer, the University of North Carolina launched a new VR software application allowing students to view and experience aspects of the college. Earlier this year, The Dyslexia Association of Singapore created a center for smart technology and is using VR as a learning tool. Similar to AI and automation, VR has unlimited possibilities in all three markets – education, business, and consumer.

VR technology can be used for meetings enabling multiple employees to collaborate from any location in the world. Digital memos appear on the AR screens with information shared via videos and game interactions. One company driving the incorporation of AR in retail and business-to-business markets is Spacee co-founded by Skip Howard. Watching Spacee grow from a small two-person startup to an internationally known tech company is exciting. Howard is also dyslexic and uses his creativity and visual thinking talents to develop technologies for Fortune 100 clients that include Wal-Mart and Intel.

The second implementation of AR is the creation of digital workspaces. David Pierce's article, *Enjoy Your New Virtual Office* in the February issue of *Wired Magazine,* described AR workstations and how our documents, files, and conversations will be interactive and completely digital. Large enterprises, such as Facebook, Microsoft, Boeing, and Bosch "are building the hardware and software for the AR workplace."

One of the best visual examples of using AR and VR in the workplace is a video blog created and produced by Sean Douglas, founder of The Codpast. At the British Dyslexia International Conference, Sean and I chatted about this book. Many of the capabilities of AR and VR discussed in this chapter are included in his video. I believe in the future, with the implementation of AR and VR, many of the traditional text-based language pain points dyslexics and neurodiverse individuals encounter will be mitigated or made obsolete.

Both VR and AR technologies are being incorporated into the workplace or as a marketing component for products and services. As these technologies are mainstreamed and used more frequently, the incorporation of VR workstations will most likely increase. The AR and VR industries are still in the early stages of development as companies determine the practical uses of these technologies. As reality technologies become interwoven in education and the workplace, a shift from relying solely on a text-based intellect will occur as visual intelligence gains importance.

Quantum Computing

The next step is quantum computing which turbocharges AI, deep learning, and automation. While attending the 2018 SXSWedu Conference, I had a thought-provoking conversation with two researchers from Stanford and a tech founder.

Our discussion evolved to the topic of quantum computing. In the future, tech companies, like Google and IBM, will have the capacity to almost instantly find solutions unavailable on classic computers. Gerd Leonhard, a leading European futurist who speaks frequently, believes quantum computing will be possible in five to seven years. Should Leonhard's estimate be correct, my son will still be in college when this technology becomes a reality. Which makes me wonder, is the career planning we're doing now already obsolete?

On January 18, 2018, Thomas Friedman's opinion piece, *While You Were Sleeping,* appeared in the *New York Times.* Friedman provided a down to earth description of the speed of quantum computing and its potential. To give you an idea of just how fast it will be, imagine driving a 1930s Model T and then the next day riding in a Telsa rocket ship. For humans, the computing speed of a quantum computer system is incomprehensible.

Joseph Campbell said it best, *"Technology cannot save us. It's only a tool."* These powerful technologies can provide a significant benefit to society. While we incorporate these systems into our world, we must be aware of the all opportunities available and the potential adverse outcomes.

Neurodiverse individuals and dyslexics are wired differently, which provides us with an alternative thinking process and worldview. A different perspective is required to maintain an ethical balance. The technologies discussed in this chapter will continue to disrupt and transform employment, our definition of work, and humanity. Within this disruption are new employment and social opportunities for individuals with dyslexia.

Chapter Two

Literacy and Language Redefined

"Never limit yourself because of others'
limited imagination."
–Mae Jemison

How will society define literacy and language in 2023 or 2030? The current definition is derived from a text-based intellect. Johannes Gutenberg perfected the printing press in the 15ᵗʰ century. Like Henry Ford did with automobiles, Gutenberg developed an assembly-line printing press that mass-produced books more efficiently and at a considerably lower cost. His invention was the catalyst for spreading knowledge and information across Europe.

Before Gutenberg's invention, only a select group of individuals associated with churches, royal families, and governments had access to printed books. As the printing press technology spread across the world, schools and businesses used a person's ability to read and write to determined their literacy and employment potential. As we know, this benchmark does not measure an individual's full capabilities especially if they are dyslexic or have a learning difference. Furthermore, as visual technologies, such as virtual and augmented reality become part of our workstations, the definition of literacy will need to be expanded to include both text and visual-based aptitude.

Digital technology is a game changer for neurodiverse individuals. Today, assistive technology offers us the ability to work alongside our peers with minimum assistance. Initially, I wrestled with this chapter. Wondering if it had a place in a book about AI, automation, employment, and creativity. The purpose of this chapter was evident as I thought about the impact of technology and the range of benefits and advantages individuals with dyslexia can offer. Initiating a discussion about how we will define literacy in the future and the use of emerging digital languages is essential. Currently, dyslexics are defined and limited by the text-based interpretation of literacy.

Today, there are dozens if not hundreds of digital tools and software applications to help individuals spell, read, and write on their mobile devices and computers. During my senior year of high school, my parents purchased a home computer. For the first time, ever, I could write school papers and the computer would spell check my work. Overnight, I became independent. No longer was I dependent on my mother, who was an AP Honors High School

English teacher, to check my spelling. The feeling of liberation was instant. As a result, I wrote more and over time developed the confidence to express my knowledge and ideas.

My son is dyslexic and uses assistive technology to read, write, spell, and audio dictate information to his mobile device and home computer. Mobile devices and computers have accessibility features enabling individuals to communicate and engage with others without using text-based skills to read and write. The computers do the work for us. Just as I am typing this chapter, I am using three different software applications to review spelling and grammar. Chrome is a click away for instant help with spelling or to verify a word.

The languages we use to communicate are evolving as well. The use of emojis as a form of image-based language is gaining traction in schools. Education conferences now include sessions about the impact of emojis and how to teach the image-based language alongside our text-based language.

New digital languages will emerge as we use images and graphics to share information and convey meaning. Infographics shared on Instagram, LinkedIn, and YouTube can provide more complex information than a text generated paragraph. As companies incorporate virtual reality workstations, how we communicate at work will continue to change as well. We use infographics and symbols to share information globally more frequently than we realize. How will society define literacy when the majority of the work is done via voice commands, typing, and movement of our mouse or hand? I believe defining literacy using a text-based intellect will become obsolete.

The definition of literacy should evolve and be based on abilities and skills congruent with our digital world. To move forward and change the perception of dyslexia and neurodiversity, we must reconsider what constitutes literacy and discuss how new digital languages will offer more ways to communicate.

Chapter Three

The Future of Work

"Talent is a slippery concept."
—Gerhard Gollwitzer, *The Joys of Drawing*

The future of work is a broad and encompassing topic. For this book, I took a macro view. My focus is on the key strengths, skills, and talents and characteristics of professionals with dyslexia. I also discuss how this skill set can provide a competitive advantage for companies and a significant benefit to government agencies. These advantages are most evident in areas that require creativity, an innovative mindset, big-picture thinking, visual intelligence, spatial reasoning, pattern recognition, and critical thinking.

In 2016, the World Economic Forum predicted by the year 2020 complex problem-solving, critical thinking, and creativity will be the top three in-demand skills. A shift in skill requirements is occurring as AI and automation consume many skilled jobs and professions that involve liner tasks such as accounting, banking, manufacturing, and finance.

Articles and books written about the future of work employment models discuss strategies for retraining employees. These strategies include reimagining tactical work components, creating future skill requirements, and checklists for retraining talent. These skills require proficiencies working in a AR and VR environment with the ability to use interactive AI workstations.

To acquire these skills requires a significant retooling for all employees even tech-savvy professionals as the global employment model undergoes a paragon shift. I believe learning these new skills is very different from 20 years ago when everyone had to learn Microsoft Office (Office). The technology today is advanced, invisible, and rapidly accelerating. In the 1990s, the learning pace was manageable with a singular focus.

The digital economy requires workers to learn unfamiliar skills. Employees must understand how AI, automation, and deep learning systems function. Employment is evolving from a one-dimensional work environment to a 3-dimensional virtual space requiring a system management work view. Based on my research, I created a futurist version of our global employment model for the year 2025.

In six and half years from now, these advanced technologies will become interwoven within our global economy. Similar to the Long Tail and Gig Economy, I believe work tasks will be granular with income derived from smaller task increments. I have a hunch that a variation of my future of work is already occurring.

Year 2025

The early stages of quantum computing are evident as companies develop processes for deploying the new technology. Talent acquisition and workplace management systems combined with AI and automation have eliminated many traditional work positions and job titles. Individuals are reclassified by their talents, skills, and experience. Resumes, grade point averages, and standardized test scores are obsolete. Students and professionals are pre-screened using a universal talent management system that uses big data to determine college placement and an individual's career placement based on natural characteristics, gaming skills, and big data assessment.

Corporate employment platform systems monitor the status of projects and open tasks to be completed within a goal determined timeframe. Employees and freelance workers can be added within minutes to a project to increase productivity or make adjustments for unexpected external events. Freelancers are provided by talent services that specialized in specific industries and skill sets.

These cognitive freelancers move from project to project during their workday. The number of hours each freelancer needs to work is calculated by their Individual Income System (IncomeS). The IncomeS determines then how much money a person needs to generate based on consumption and subscription fees. Workers' earnings are determined by the scope of the project, skill level, and experience. Talent platforms enable companies to engage a flexible talent pool from anywhere in the world.

Human resource and management platforms enhanced by deep learning, led by industry leader, SuccessFactors by SAP, created the disruption resulting in a redefinition of employment. Individuals work on projects and tasks in team hives or individually depending on the assigned initiatives. Managers are obsolete and replaced with system coordinators or project collaborators. Projects range in size from small internal strategies to developing new products or finding solutions for clients.

These platform systems identify, in real time using predictive analytics, which tasks or projects need to be completed first. Professionals who possess big picture visual intellect skills are responsible for coordinating and managing project components. These project captains motivate and lead innovation teams, manage the human element and emotional intelligence, while solving any problems that arise from AI miscalculations or human errors.

While keeping this futuristic employment model in mind, let's return to 2018.

Dyslexic Employees and Professionals
Five Key Future of Work Strengths

Based on my research and interviews, these are the five-key future of work areas where dyslexics can provide a significant benefit based on their skills, strengths, and talents.

- Visionary: leadership, solving existing and future complex problems, and envisioning innovative products and services yet to be developed.

- Creativity: designing system workflows for managing a diverse talent pool that includes humans, robots, and AI software.

- Visual Intelligence: understanding, designing, and managing the use VR and AR in the educational, business, and entertainment industries.

- Spatial Reasoning and big picture thinking: exceling in the areas of cybertech, cybersecurity, big data, and data analytics.

- Entrepreneurship: launching fluid businesses to provide products and services based on the future of work employment model.

Areas of Concern

In the September 2018 edition of *Fast Company*, cover story, "Moneyball For Business", written by Aaron Carr, discusses the gamification of talent acquisition, driven by employee matching startups. These startups combine neuroscience with deep learning to develop systems to select high achievers from the candidate pool.

One of the startups mentioned in Carr's article was Pymetrics. Frida Polli, an MIT graduate, co-founded the company with a classmate. Her goal is to find a more efficient method for matching potential candidates with employers. I contracted Polli and a senior programmer to learn more about the system they created and if characteristics of dyslexics and neurodiverse individuals were included in the software. As of the publish date, I have not received a response from the company.

Pymetrics is one of the first of a new wave of talent matching startups working to disrupt HR and how companies find and place new employees. My hunch is the disruption created by these startups will have a ripple effect on higher education and k-12.

From 2012 through 2014, while writing *You Posted What!?* I noticed similar parallels in my research. The impact of the talent acquisition platforms will increase the granular measurement and tracking of every workflow detail of employees and further divide human talent into very defined categories and segments. From an AI perspective, every tiny detail of work will be labeled, measured, and analyzed by deep learning systems, providing HR and management with a wealth of information.

Once an individual fails to learn a new skill or gain critical job experience, the system will shift them to a different job area. The irony of these systems is the coding foundation on which they are built most likely includes unconscious biases, which will bypass neurodiverse individuals. These software platforms are designed to locate the cognitive elite in the most efficient means possible to increase productivity both for the company and employee. Understanding how these systems are coded enables companies to develop outlier programs to find dyslexic professionals.

Chapter Four

Disrupting Employment Perceptions

"You never change things by fighting the existing realities. To change something, build a new model that makes the existing model obsolete."
—R. Buckminster Fuller

Early one morning, I made the mistake of checking LinkedIn before I had coffee. A post written by an HR consultant listed signs to help fellow professionals identify dyslexic employees. The list started with common weaknesses. The consultant never mentioned the strengths often associated with individuals who are dyslexic.

My immediate thoughts were, "Can we for once focus on our strengths instead of our weaknesses?" Every time I read an article, spelling comes up almost immediately as an identifier for dyslexic students and employees.

With the use of spell check and predictive auto fill software programs using misspelling as a criterion for dyslexia is quickly becoming antiquated. As we adapted to digital technology and the Internet, our writing style has evolved to be more casual than previous generations. Dozens of mistakes appear daily in the digital content as individuals spend less time editing and checking for grammatical errors.

So why do we continue to base our perception of intelligence on the ability to read and spell when advanced technologies will most likely make these skills less important in the future?

Since the development of mechanical tools, thousands of years ago, technology has always driven progress, eliminating what was obsolete while creating new opportunities. Studying history provides us with a perspective of how technological advancements have shaped humanity and our work from the printing press to the iPhone.

Neurodiverse individuals created many of the previous technologies and systems we use today. Before the invention of the microchip and digital technology, our world was confined to a text-based measurement for intelligence. Work and success were determined by how fast you could read, which words you could spell, and your language processing speed.

As digital technology becomes interwoven in the workplace many of the coveted skills initially developed during the first phase of the Industrial Revolution will become less important.

Most dyslexics feel at home using a wide range of digital technologies to mitigate their deficiencies and enhance their strengths. There are dozens of digital tools I can access within minutes to complete my work.

To change the perception of how individuals with dyslexia are perceived in the world, we must first be recognized for our strengths and determine if any of our weaknesses are job-related. If so, then develop a plan to manage or mitigate these weaknesses. Remember, all employees have weaknesses that can impact their work to varying degrees.

How to Change the Perception of Dyslexia in the Workplace

Corporate Workshops

Conducting corporate dyslexia workshops to educate all employees from the executives to the new hires is crucial. A company's long-term sustainability depends upon its ability to develop, plan, and implement programs designed to create an inclusive and multi-diverse culture.

A recent study by the Institute of Economic and Social Research reinforces the need for individuals with dyslexia. The study, "urges employers to consider the numerous positive attributes associated with neurodiverse individuals from creativity, persistence, to the possession of visual, spatial and lateral thinking skills." For everyone to benefit, training programs should include specific information based on common strengths and talents, and then demonstrate how these strengths are related to practice areas within the company.

For example, showcase the benefits of spatial and big-picture thinking for managing systems and recognizing trends within the mountains of big data. Often, educators who are asked to provide training may be limited in their knowledge of how advanced technologies are transforming work, information about new emerging employment opportunities, and how talent characteristics of dyslexia align with AR and VR.

When developing corporate workshops, enlist feedback and information from consultants and employees who are dyslexic and neurodiverse.

- Ask how they would design an internal workshop to educate their peers and senior management about dyslexia.

- What information would benefit everyone?

- What strategies would they share?

- What assistive technologies do they need?

- Provide recommended list of reading, spelling, and language software applications that are compatible with the company's network.

During one of my interviews, an employee at a large defense contractor stated, "It would be amazing if all companies had a boilerplate of accommodations for dyslexics. Ready to go. The document would be for employees, published within the company so that individuals who are afraid to speak up could still benefit." In the final editing phase of this book, I added two short chapters for HR departments and managers. In Chapter Ten, I created a dyslexia workplace checklist template.

Open Door Policy

It's 2018, and I continue to receive emails from professionals, located in multiple countries, who are afraid to disclose their dyslexia to management and HR. These individuals are seeking assistive tech support or similar accommodations to be more productive at work. Having these tools available is similar to providing employees with ongoing training or new computers to improve their work experience. In my mind, there is *no difference* between providing assistive tech to dyslexic professionals and providing software upgrades to help the sales team reach their goals.

With so many assistive technology software applications and devices available, neurodiverse employees should not have to fear to ask for assistive technology solutions. Secondly, ensuring dyslexic professionals have mentors is equally important. Regardless of the matter, having employees afraid to ask for support should not be occurring in 2018. Companies must commit to developing multi-diverse inclusive programs that become part of the company's culture. Diversity generates different viewpoints which drives innovation.

Second, educate employers and HR teams about our strengths and talent with a focus on new employment opportunities created by AI and automation. Every dyslexic can contribute to our global society when they are provided assistive tech tools, receive internal support, and are considered for job positions that enable them to use their strengths and talents.

Within the dyslexia community, we must shift our focus to our strengths and be mindful of the words we use to describe our challenges. When we constantly talk about our weaknesses, instead of creating a balance in the conversation, we only reinforce the less than favorable image in the workplace. Dyslexia is gaining awareness in more countries around the world, educating individuals about the strengths and weaknesses must occur together. I recommended always discussing strengths first followed by listing areas where we encounter challenges.

Dyslexia is global. When everyone works together from the executive level to HR managers and individuals in the dyslexia community, we have the power to change the perception of dyslexia from solely as a weakness to a powerhouse of strength and talent.

Chapter Five

Operating in Your Areas of Strengths

"Some look at things that are, and ask why. I dream of things that never were and ask why not?"
-Playwrite George Bernard Shaw

Six years ago, I connected with Andrea Traslvaina, who is the Director of Global Recruiting for Whole Foods Market in Austin, Texas. He said, "the most important thing a person can do during their career is to align their innate talents, experience, and strengths."

During our various chats, he talked about how to build a career foundation to ensure long-term sustainability. Traslvaina said, "you must find your career *sweet spot.*" That is when a person focuses on gaining experiences and new skills to strengthen their innate talents. In a nutshell, he said to succeed in our careers, we must always operate in our areas of strength.

His advice seems simple. When I speak at a conference or event, I ask the audience if they can identify their innate talent. Each time about 20% of the group will nod their heads or say a quiet yes. We spend years building our careers. Moving from different employment positions to gain more experience and increase our income. I know from personal experience taking positions outside your innate talent causes frustration and can do more damage long term.

For dyslexic professionals, I believe it is essential to spend time thinking about your innate talents and strengths. Our natural talents are evident when we are young. We engage in activities that are natural and easy. When I was a kid living in the Houston area, I would run outside with my hairbrush mic to report the weather or I would write short stories and plays. Every activity I did in my free time had a creative element. I was always creating or inventing something. When I was a teen, I started a babysitting business with weekly retainer customers.

The days of "reporting the weather" as a kid translated into public speaking. The creativity has evolved into career positions in corporate marketing, product development, and writing books. The babysitting was the initial foundation for entrepreneurship. Last year, I came across research conducted by Dr. Michael Ryan, who specializes in working with dyslexics. He found "the dyslexic's strengths and weakness may be closely related." He noted a young graduate student who was studying advanced calculus yet could not remember phone numbers. Included in his article and research were multiple examples where the dyslexic experienced innate talent and weakness in the same area.

If your innate talents are not obvious, spend time thinking about your childhood. Your talents may reside alongside your dyslexia. When our natural skills are interwoven within the dyslexia, it can be a very frustrating experience as others see the weakness first instead of the talent. Educators and family members may attempt to steer you towards a different profession. Assistive technology software and devices are enabling us to outsource these weaknesses.

Two years ago, I read Carson Tate's book, *Work Simply.* Tate does an excellent job describing the different productivity styles. I recommend purchasing a copy of the book or checking it out of the library. Every visualizer she mentioned is neurodiverse or dyslexic. Reading through the book was refreshing and a reminder to delegate work areas where I am least productive. These tasks include repetitive responsibilities, slow pace, rigid framework, and unnecessary details. Almost half of the book pages are tagged or marked. After reading the book, I restructured my work days to focus on the most important matters at the beginning of the week. Especially, for the required repetitive tasks I must complete. My ability to remain focused and patient with tedious tasks is easier on

Monday and Tuesday than late Thursday or Friday afternoon when my dyslexic brain is screaming for creative recess!

I believe it is essential to develop a career strategy that combines innate talents, experience, and dyslexia strengths. In the margin of the page or on your computer, list your innate talents and strengths.

- Does your professional expertise align with your strengths?

- Did you list the common characteristics associated with dyslexia such as creativity, big-picture thinking, pattern recognition, and system thinking?

- In your current position are you using these skills?

- Are there positions at your company that would be a better fit?

- Is your career aligned with your innate talents?

- Have you combined your abilities with your dyslexia strengths?

So many times, the perception of others creates roadblocks during our careers. In the past, I have traveled down the wrong path because family members thought I should pursue

50

a career completely outside my skill area. The lost time is frustrating. You know your capabilities. You know your strengths and how dyslexia can turbo charge your career and when to outsource the weaknesses. To build a sustainable career, working in your areas of strength is a must.

Traslvaina's advice is golden. He coaches his staff to always build upon their greatest assets. *"Take your talent ladder and place it on the right wall. That way you will always be working your way upward towards your goal."* Anything less is a misallocation of our most precious resource – *time.*

Chapter Six

Creativity and Innovation

"The question is, who is interested in creativity? And my answer is that practically everybody is. This interest is no longer confined to psychologists or psychiatrists. Now it has become a question of national and international policy as well."
-Abraham Maslow, *The Farther Reaches of Human Nature*

The most powerful competitive advantage in the Machine Age is human creativity and ingenuity. Advanced systems including AI, automation, and quantum computing will always lack the ability to daydream and use an organic means to imagine something new. I believe humans, especially individuals who have perfected their creativity skills and talents, will always have an advantage.

To daydream, to connect unrelated dots, human feelings, and everything else into a concise thought or idea only occurs within the human brain. The foundation of everything we do, design, build is derived from creative thinking. Dyslexics are known for their creative and innovative abilities. I believe we possess these talents for two reasons. First, the generic design of our brains places more emphases on the visual, perceptual mode and areas where creativity resides. Second, since the time we were toddlers, our brains are constantly (24/7/365) developing creative workarounds and solutions to adapt, work, communicate, and live in a society dominated by cultural norms founded on a text-based intelligence.

So Why Are Dyslexics So Creative?

"We are what we repeatedly do. Excellence then is not an act, but a habit." –Aristotle

As humans, we're still amazed and often baffled as to how creativity happens. Numerous research articles, TEDx Talks, and books discuss how our brains generate new ideas or experience creative flow. Most children, when given free play time will display creativity in developing games, building new toys or picking up random objects like a large stick and then imagining it's a flag or sword.

Most dyslexics have hundreds if not thousands of creative, innovative thoughts a day. These thoughts include problem-solving, developing a workaround or envisioning an idea

54

or product. Thinking creatively is both a survival technique and a continuous function of our brains. On the weekends, we drive around our neighborhoods redesigning houses as a form of relaxation. Our creativity neurons are in constant use from the moment we are awake until we fall asleep.

Any action humans perform repeatedly and then use new knowledge and skills to enhance the repeated activity will at some point become an expert or be considered talented in the area of practice. Constantly using our creativity in various environments combined with unpredictable situations provides us an advantage in the creativity department. At times, I take my creativity for granted, because I use the talent all the time.

My son is dyslexic, which means innovative thinking and creative outburst are our norm. I use my creativity continually to problem solve and produce ideas. I am always surprised when clients, say "Wow, you're so creative!", or "That's a creative thought, how did you think of that?" Generally, my dyslexic brain deadpans, "This is what I do all day long, just another day at the office, kinda thing."

I receive emails from dyslexic professionals who express their frustrations when managers are unsure of how to handle their creative ideas or input. Which is ironic since everywhere I read, companies are developing creative and innovative initiatives. Recently, Texas A & M University launched the Creativity, Innovation, Problem Solving Degree plan. The

School of Business established the degree plan to help encourage creative thinking and innovation. Every time I read or hear of companies or universities seeking creative, innovative, problem-solvers, I think why not just say *"seeking dyslexics to imagine, create, and build."*

Hiring Creative Dyslexic Employees and Contractors

The future of work is evolving towards a human-machine integration and collaboration. Companies will need to find a way to differentiate their products and services in the marketplace by building teams of highly creative, innovative employees, or freelance workers. Erik Brynjofsson and Andrew McAfee have written two books about the Fourth Phase of the Industrial Revolution. Throughout their second book, *The Second Machine Age,* they frequently mentioned the importance of creativity and non-structured problem-solving, "Investments in human capital will be increasingly important as routine tasks become automated and the need for human creativity increases."

The need for human creativity screams from articles, blog posts, and websites. Where are these creative workers we so desperately need? HR software platforms coded to find the cookie cutter cogitative elite often miss the creative dyslexics as we are outliers. We are the non-box checkers in the bunch.

As Seth Godin so eloquently pointed out in his book *The Icarus Deception*, when he discussed why a high percentage of dyslexics are successful entrepreneurs. He wrote, "I'm not sure it's because of their mental differences give them a performance edge. No, I think it's because of their outlier tendencies made it clear to them early on that they would be less likely to be picked. Less likely to be at the top of their class or chosen by the fancy college or recruiter by P & G. Precisely because they didn't fit in, they had little choice but to pick themselves. And once that choice is made, it becomes a habit."

We are used to being on the outside and are selective on how we approach employment. Each job involves a series of creative workaround strategies at various levels depending on the position and demands of the job. As more companies use gamification to find employees, I am curious about the impact on dyslexics in the workplace. My hunch is that dyslexics may have an advantage due to our strong spatial reasoning and visual intelligence skills. Another possible outcome is that while dyslexics are playing the game, they will think of ways to build a better software application. Along with our different way of thinking, we also possess maverick tendencies.

When companies are seeking creative, innovative individuals, i.e., dyslexics, its best to develop a recruiting program designed to include our outlier characteristics. When seeking to hire internally, ask referrals from dyslexic employees. During college recruitment, sponsor a Fireside

Chat at the Student Services office. For example, think coffee and Post-It Notes break use Post-It Notes to brainstorm ideas on how student candidates can use their skills for open positions. Ask for feedback about how they can use their creativity and innovation insight to benefit the company. To find dyslexic candidates, companies and recruiters will need to think outside the box.

Dyslexic Professionals
How to Use Your Creativity at Work

For dyslexic professionals, use your creative skills to envision how your abilities can benefit the employer or company you have targeted for future employment.

Remember, because we generate ideas all the time, create a job idea notebook and select the best five each month to share with your work team or manager. When I worked for FINRA (regulatory agency for NASDAQ), I was promoted to the design team to develop an internal software system to reduce the number of redundant tasks performed during routine audits. Instead of fire hosing the ideas to my boss, I drafted a summary, created mockups, and then explained how automating the process would increase our efficiency. By taking the time to compile my thoughts with examples, the ideas caught the attention of management. I was promoted to the design team to help develop an agency-wide automation program. Here's a list of questions to help you brainstorm. Think about how to transform your creative energy into tangible results. I included several questions for individuals seeking a new job and college graduates.

- Research and learn about the business, market, and products.

- Consider how disruptive technology could impact and transform the industry. What hidden opportunities do you see?

- From a systems management perceptive, consider how you can use creative thinking and spatial abilities to envision employment models to incorporate automated systems, humans, and robots.

- When using big-picture problem-solving skills, think about how you can create solutions for payroll, accounting, finance or other practice areas. Think about how you can solve an old problem with new technology.

- Think about robots, from education to the consumer market. Consider mass customization of personal use robots.

- Consider how you can use your creative, problem-solving skills to anticipate future problems and trends.

  o Many of the opportunities becoming available in the Machine Age are hidden within the disruption.

- Consider contacting AR and VR emerging tech companies for career opportunities.

- Identify persistent problems your company needs solved? Start a journal and capture your ideas.

Keep in mind, finding a career and employment position that allows you to use creativity may take time to find the best fit. Expressing our creative energy is important. Every person interviewed for this book mentioned the need for a creative outlet. Remember to schedule time in your day for a creative project outside of work.

Dyslexics as the New Chief Innovation Officer

In a 2014 Harvard Business Review article, Alessandro Di Fiore, described the role of a Chief Innovation Officer (CIO). Di Fiore listed seven key roles: promoting innovative and creative thinking, developing programs to build innovation skills, support innovation teams across the company, look for new opportunities, conduct idea-generating sessions, funding for innovation, and protecting of potential ideas.

The function of the CIO as described by Di Fiore is to create "a more innovation friendly organizational environment." Recruiting, grooming, and helping dyslexics become CIO's for companies seems to be a no-brainer. When reviewing the responsibilities listed, many of the tasks listed are in our areas of strength. Leaders must have an innate knowledge of how to build an innovative culture.

Joseph Pistrui is a Professor of Entrepreneurial Management and Innovation at the IE Business School in Madrid. He lectures and writes about innovation. Pistrui's article, *The Future of Human Work is Imagination, Creativity, and Strategy,* was included in the January 2018 edition of the *Harvard Business Review.* He discussed the potential impact of machines on the future of work. AI machines are focused on tactical tasks, think accounting, bank tellers, and quality control workers. Jobs that manage highly tactical tasks have a higher probability of being automated in the next five to ten years. Where "work that requires a high degree of imagination, creative analysis and strategic thinking is harder to automate."

As I have discussed in this chapter, dyslexics are creative because we use this skill to problem-solve. With a new sense of urgency for finding and capturing creativity as a competitive advantage, companies will need to design environments that allow employees to daydream and consider many ideas while at the same time maintaining a profitable business. Tech companies are known for allowing employees to "tinker" with ideas or inventions knowing within these thousands of ideas the next iPhone or Post-It Note product will emerge.

Professor Bishop, futurist and former professor at the University of Houston, wrote about how to teach the future, and how to prepare students for 2020 and beyond. Two essential mutually beneficial skills mentioned were critical thinking and creativity. In his book, *Teaching About the Future*, he mentioned a 1993 study conducted to learn how "some of history's greatest creative thinkers found that what appear to be sudden bursts in creative genius were in fact the product of years of hard work and study."

Dyslexics understand innately the process behind creative thinking, we experience hundreds of original thoughts a day and quickly dismiss or save the ones we think have value. Many of us use journals or digital means to capture our thinking. Creativity is a skill and process that requires discipline and work. I have dozens of journals and review them for ideas when seeking a solution.

Significant creative breakthroughs occur over time, piecing together separate parts and viewing the world through a different lens. The critical question for creativity today is – *are we*

*willing to do the hard work, be patient, and allow
time for the great ideas to emerge?*

Impact of AI on Innovation and Creativity

Is there an inverse relationship between AI
and innovation? I say "yes" that the more we use
AI, the less innovative and creative humans will
become.

As we continue to outsource our brains to
AI from a range of tasks both simple and complex,
we become passive participants. Using software
to find the cognitive elite, clean our inbox, and
manage the IoT (Internet of Things) in our homes
removes us from deep learning gained when we
encounter problems. The more removed we are
from the problem-solving process, the more
complacent we become. Our skills are
strengthened when we are faced with
challenging, at times very frustrating situations.
Workarounds and solutions are created to
remove pain points. The majority of the business
associates I know believe AI will free our minds to
be more creative and solve problems.

However, by removing the necessary steps
from the process, the foundation on which
problem-solving is built is also eliminated. Any
feedback provided to the individual feels shallow
as there is no corresponding reference point. Nor
does the individual have a previous challenge to
use as a reference point for understanding how

the mistake occurred. When individuals lack the basic foundation for problem-solving they lose the ability to envision a solution.

Creativity is the root of all problem-solving. When we are removed from the problem-solving process, we lose the ability to gain critical skills needed to adequately solve more advanced complex problems. Last month, I was in Starbucks picking up a pound of coffee and asked to have the coffee ground. The employee didn't know how to put the coffee in the machine. The whole process took three employees to complete. Yes, this is partly Starbuck's fault for not training their staff. The individual had no mental reference point to intuitively solve the problem which was the most concerning part of the interaction. She stared at the machine, with her hand on her phone desperately wanting to Google the answer. Another employee quickly demonstrated how to grind coffee. How technology is creating gaps in our problem-solving skills is a topic for another book! I believe dyslexics, when tasked to solve problems, have a competitive advantage. I am concerned that with frequent use of AI, human creativity will be greatly diminished if not lost. I encourage fellow dyslexics and creative thinkers to protect this unique human ability.

As enterprises, organizations, and universities recognize the importance of creative thinking, the demand for individuals who are creative problem-solvers will increase. I close this chapter with another quote from Brynjolfsson and McAffee as I believe building an environment that encourages human creativity is an absolute must.

Eric Brynjolfsson and Andrew McAffee - *The Second Machine Age.*

"We've never seen a truly creative machine, or an entrepreneurial one, or an innovative one. Ideation in its many forms is an area today where humans have a comparable advantage over machines. Ideation, creativity, and innovation are often described as 'thinking outside the box' and this characterization indicates another large and reasonably sustainable advantage of human over digital labor."

Chapter Seven

Visual Intelligence and Spatial Thinking

"Spatials often 'see' ideas in a 3-dimension like computer animation with depth. They look through both real and imagined space to see the whole of something and to check out the relationships and connections. This creates an inner territory to explore."
-Visual Spatial Research Organization

The majority of the articles written about the characteristics of dyslexic individuals generally focus on three advantages: problem-solving, creativity, and innovation. Visual intelligence and spatial reasoning is mentioned some, but not enough. Thomas West's book, *Seeing What Others Cannot See*, discusses the hidden advantages visual thinkers possess. Dyslexics use their visual intelligence and spatial abilities to solve problems.

A creative idea is problem-solving. Finding solutions doesn't occur in a vacuum. It is a process, requiring time to observe the whole environment surrounding the problem visually. A couple of years ago, I stumbled across an interesting book, *Drawing on the Artist Within* by Betty Edwards. Within the brown-tinged pages were Edward's research, observations, and thoughts about creativity and problem-solving. She believed creative individuals didn't wait for problems to occur. Instead creative people "actively searched out and discovered problems to solve that no one else had perceived." (The quote's tense was modified for consistency.)

Keep her phrase "no one else perceived" in your mind while reading this chapter. To find what no one else can perceive or notice is a significant advantage. AI, automation, deep learning, and big data are transforming work, automating linear tasks, and generating solutions. The difficult part for companies is finding the important subtle trends, patterns, and problems within the massive digital ecosystem.

Because the digital platforms and software systems used today are similar in design and function, securing a competitive niche is intensifying. Every single aspect of work and engagement is measured and analyzed. Companies are at risk of missing important information when employees stare into the digital dashboard believing all the answers reside within the data.

Companies, organizations, and government agencies need neurodiverse professionals to find **the "digital (or human) needle in the haystack"** buried in these data-heavy digital platforms. As the future of work evolves, dyslexics will serve as visual architects designing and monitoring interactions within digital work systems while searching for patterns or problems not perceived by others. We're like the McAffee or Cisco system running in the background, catching seemingly unrelated *non-important* bits of data. We know from a gut feeling the opposite is true. When these dots of information are connected, the results are important, and in some cases, very important.

Explaining how we find the "digital needle in the haystack" can be difficult as the dyslexic brain is elusive. Hidden patterns do not appear immediately or on command. Dyslexics discover trends while mentally wondering across the landscape visually feasting on information, allowing curiosity to lead us into dark pathways, or striking up conversations with individuals outside our industry or profession. We're hunting for anomalies or "backing into" a process.

When working backward, also known as reverse engineering, the learning experience is different. While moving in reverse, important questions arise, an idea may emerge, new ways to design the process may appear, or we may find a malware bug.

In other words, we're able to view an old process from a new perspective. Our habit of working backward explains how we can look at the IKEA box and build a piece of furniture without written instructions. The entire process of finding hidden trends or backing into problems is conceived visually in our minds in a 3-dimensional format. Our thoughts and ideas are mentally displayed like mini Vemo or YouTube videos. The dyslexic brain's ability to run multiple problem-solving options and competing views at the same time as it works to uncover a solution, design a product, or find a missing piece of information is a competitive edge. The entire process is natural and instantaneous.

For dyslexic professionals, I believe the opportunities available in the cybertech and cybersecurity industries will continue to increase in both the private and government sectors. On September 21, 2014, an article in the Telegraph, announced the recruitment and employment of dyslexic and neurodiverse individuals by GCHQ, the U.K. government intelligence agency. The article quoted an IT specialist with GCHQ and discussed the advantages of dyslexics. He stated, "what people don't realize is that people with neuro diversity usually have a 'spikyskills' profile, which means that certain skill areas will be below par and others may be well above. My spatial-perception awareness and creativity is in the top 1% of my peer group."

Four years later, the GCHQ granted Sean Douglas of The Codpast an interview. Douglas met with several employees who discussed how their dyslexia was an advantage for their job. In the U.S. there are unconfirmed rumors within the education community that a large number of dyslexics are employed at various government agencies. I contacted the Dallas Federal Bureau of

Investigation office for verification and have yet not received a response. In the private sector, one of the leading cybersecurity firms Cyberreason was co-founded by a dyslexic entrepreneur, named Lior Div. In multiple media interviews, Div discussed how his dyslexia contributed to a career path in cybertech.

In addition to cybertech, big data and data analytics are two industries also seeking neurodiverse professionals. Daniel Goleman, the author of *Emotional Intelligence*, stated, "just one cognitive ability distinguished star performers from average: pattern recognition, the 'big picture' thinking that allows leaders to pick out meaningful trends from a welter of information around them and to think strategically far into the future."

A holistic approach is required to find hidden meaning within mountains of data. Dyslexics are visual big picture thinkers. We intuitively simplify large amounts of data into a concise meaning. Our brains hunt for valuable information and toss the rest.

A majority of the Tier 1 consulting firms and Fortune 500 companies are designing programs to hire individuals who have autism or Asperger syndrome. I believe these programs need to be modified to include neurodiverse individuals who have dyslexia and ADHD. The World Economic Forum published Gavin Patternson's, BT Group CEO, article on January 19, 2018. Patternson joined the list of leaders discussing the need for hiring employees who possess creative problem-solving skills, especially in the area of data science and cybertech.

The third area for new employment opportunities are in augmented and virtual reality. I believe VR technology has the most potential to make an impact from providing alternative learning tools for dyslexic students to offering new job creation. Dyslexics are known for their creative design talent. When combining creativity and VR technologies, the job prospects for dyslexics increase. I believe most dyslexics will find working in the AR and VR industries and using AR workspaces, familiar, as these technologies mirror our visual thinking process.

Before I close this chapter, I would like to mention the use of spatial reasoning to find solutions in the areas of scientific research and development. About a third of the emails I receive are from scientists, chemists, and biologists who talk about how they use their spatial reasoning to solve problems or uncover new scientific discoveries critical to their employer's or university's research and development department. The emails have similar stories such as co-workers having a difficult time understanding their thought process. Every article I have read about dyslexic scientists, who were award a Noble Prize, the individuals attribute their spatial reasoning and visual thinking abilities as the reason for the achievements.

Spatial reasoning and visual thinking opportunities will materialize for dyslexics when companies understand the value for hiring dyslexics for positions that require these skills and talents. Educating career and job placement centers about these new employment areas is also equally as important.

Chapter Eight

Entrepreneurship is a Mindset

"Only those who will risk going too far can possibly find out how far it is possible to go."
— *T.S. Elliot*

Julie Logan, a professor at the Case School of Business in London, England, conducted a study to assess if there was a link between dyslexia and business ownership. She shared her findings in a 2008 academic abstract. Her research included surveying business owners and corporate managers in the U.S. and the U.K. to determine how many were dyslexic or identified themselves as being dyslexic. Corporate managers were added to the survey as a control group.

Logan discovered 35% of the entrepreneurs in the U.S. were dyslexic and only 15% of corporate managers identified themselves as being dyslexic. Within the dyslexic group, 23% reported themselves as being highly dyslexic or extremely dyslexic. Dyslexic founders were more likely to own several companies, employ more staff, and delegate more than non-dyslexic business owners. Many dyslexic entrepreneurs "preferred the early stages of business startup when they could control their environment." The study asked participants to rank their skills. The top skills listed by the dyslexics were excellent oral communication, delegation, creativity, and spatial awareness.

One of the more interesting findings from the study was that dyslexic entrepreneurs indicated they were influenced by mentors (family members) or non-dyslexic entrepreneurs. Over 80% of the dyslexics surveyed stated they faced adversity in their childhood. Logan's study was the inspiration for my 2015 TEDx Talk, *Dyslexia 2.0: The Gift of Innovation and Entrepreneurial Mind* and my book *Dyslexia's Competitive Edge*. The purpose of this book was to create a resource that I wished had been available when I was in college that showcased our strengths and shared strategies from fellow dyslexics.

I believe entrepreneurship is part DNA, part environmental, and part personal characteristics. Grit, tenacity, and perseverance are three of the most valued traits and the most difficult to teach. The majority of dyslexics obtained these traits by junior high school. Every day at school is a test of the fail fast pivot Lean Startup model (an entrepreneurial model for launching companies). We quickly learn how to manage adversity, bounce back from setbacks, remain persistent in finding solutions, and see problems or structures from a different perspective.

Entrepreneurship is a mindset, especially in the dyslexia community. Most dyslexic students start a business. In 2013, I created Jr. Startup, a Meetup group, for young entrepreneurs ages 8 – 14. My son helped form the group. Jr. Startup met monthly and was a forum for students to discuss and develop their ideas. The majority of the students that attended the group meetings were neurodiverse. Creating entrepreneurial groups for dyslexic students is vital for two reasons. The groups provide guidance during idea development and mentor support. As advanced technologies continue to disrupt employment, the number of self-employed individuals will increase. The majority of the employment predictions estimate between 35% and 43% of the workforce will be self-employed by 2025.

Dyslexics' entrepreneurial strengths, I predict, will increase in demand in three areas. First, enterprises and organizations will seek individuals who are naturally creative and innovative due to intense global competition. Companies must innovate to avoid becoming obsolete and have two choices: purchase startups or develop new concepts internally. Enterprises that develop in-house entrepreneurial programs can gain an advantage by hiring dyslexics and neurodiverse individuals. Or companies can fund dyslexic entrepreneurs. Tactical aspects of developing an idea into a viable product or service can be learned. However, the essence of understanding the big picture, delegating, and building strong teams is difficult to duplicate. As I have written and said, hundreds of times, the last competitive edge against the machines is human creativity and ingenuity which is the foundation for entrepreneurship.

The second area is developing internal programs and initiatives where entrepreneurship is used as a mindset for complex problem-solving. Companies and organizations assemble neurodiverse teams with the mission of combining technology and human ingenuity for solution development.

The third area is creating a forum for community leaders for micro-entrepreneurs, business owners, and freelancers. As the Gig Economy grows, and companies shift to using a hybrid workforce the number of individuals who are self-employed will increase. The grassroots hybrid employment community will need leaders to build both formal and informal avenues for sharing information and resources.

Leadership is mentioned frequently as a common trait among dyslexic professionals and business owners. Our team building talents are derived from intuition and backed by our ease of delegating tasks to build a team of complementary talent. I encourage dyslexic business owners to build informal groups and host coffee chat sessions to increase awareness and create an infrastructure we'll need in th

Chapter Nine

First Day Onbording Dyslexia Style

"Everyone has something valuable to bring to the table."
—Richard Branson

In the past year, I have received numerous emails from dyslexic employees seeking help and advice on how to obtain more support from their employers in the U.S. and Europe. Along with these emails were comments made by inclusion consultants about the ongoing perception of dyslexia as a "charity" in the workplace.

As a result of the emails and conversations, I added Chapters 9 and 10 to the original manuscript. All employees, especially individuals who are neurodiverse, should receive support from their employer and HR department. I hear from recruiters, who beg for individuals who are creative, big picture (outside the box) thinkers while at the same time often dismissing individuals who think differently. One hiring manager said, "They won't touch this (dyslexia) with a ten-foot pole." Or they danced around the "dyslexia" like it was a hot potato. This type of dancing drains everyone's energy. Dyslexics must be recognized for their beneficial strengths and talents first, before the perception of dyslexia changes in the workplace. *Onboarding Dyslexia Style* is an edited version of a blog I wrote earlier this year.

Onboarding Dyslexia Style

Starting a new job or project is stressful. For most of us, the process brings back memories of starting new schools and having to navigate an unfamiliar territory with no established friendships or informal office networks. For neurodiverse professionals, starting a new job can present additional challenges as we work to assess and quickly adapt to a new work environment.

My dyslexic brain has a difficult time remembering peoples' names. I am unable to hear the individual sounds to pronounce their name phonically. The first day becomes an interesting obstacle course of encountering challenges and then quickly creating workarounds. My brain switches into survival mode to remember vital information and people, similar to traveling in a foreign country. We take note of the subtle interpersonal dynamics and informal political structures. In our minds, we create a visual view of workflows and informal processes while creating a quick assessment of strategic team members.

Dyslexics quickly assess the lay of the land to devise workplace strategies to match our new environment. When I worked in corporate, I rarely thought about the process because it naturally occurred after years of developing adaptive strategies. The first day can be summarized as creative problem-solving on steroid

Accessibility Settings for Computer and Office Equipment

If your department does not have a technology request checklist for neurodiverse employees – create one. No fancy form required, just a list of computer settings the new hire would like added to their computer, company phone, and office equipment that they will frequently use.

Having access to internal grammar and spell check software programs is a necessity for most individuals with dyslexia. I receive emails from professionals seeking to use Grammarly at work.

However, their employer's firewall prevents access. I exchanged messages with one of the co-founders of Grammarly, Alex Shevchenko. He wrote, "We are working on custom solutions for larger corporations that would like to enable Grammarly for their employees. For the time being, the best solution is to use the web version of the Grammarly Editor which should not interfere with firewalls."

Important

Send the checklist to the new hire a week or two before their start date to allow IT time to create their settings and test the software. Having, access to a computer, email, and internal systems on the first day is crucial.

Necessary Paperwork

If possible, send the required employment paperwork to the new hire a couple of days prior to their state date. Having extra time to complete the forms without feeling rushed helps reduce first day stress enabling dyslexics to focus on important matters such as meeting team members and learning the company's systems.

Company Welcome Mat

For a while, on LinkedIn, everyone was posting their First Day office swag photos. During the first day on the job, employees are accessing the company as much as fellow team members are checking out the new hire. Businesses that welcome new hires and have team members available generally have a lower turn overrate. No one likes walking into a new place and feeling unwelcomed. Before the first day, assign a team buddy or someone from HR to meet the new hire and offer support during the day.

Set up their workstation with a computer, login information, and supplies. Be sure to include a stack of different color Post-It Notes, a whiteboard, and Sharpies. If possible, create an infographic of the team with their photos and a short bio. The more visual information provided, the better. For example, for a team infographic: Lauren – the guru of marketing, dog's name is Champ, likes to eat Indian food on Fridays. Josh – tech of the group, bikes every day, loves to hike.

Infographics create visual connections to remember names and job functions, plus they provide information for small talk topics. Creating a relaxed and welcoming atmosphere for all hires is essential. Adding these extra tweaks for dyslexic new employees helps reduce first day stress so they can focus on what matters most – *their new jobs.*

Chapter Ten

HR Team Advice and The Dyslexia Checklist

"I believe success is achieved by ordinary people with extraordinary determination."
—Zig Zinger

The second most requested type of support from professionals with dyslexia is having mentorships and access to a universal checklist of all the technology tools and software applications, and non-tech accommodations provided by the company.

Corporate Dyslexia Groups

John Levell, a former EY Associate Partner in the London office, co-founded Diversity and Inclusivity Staff Network. Levell was one of the first to create a company-sponsored dyslexia happy hour event. The group continues to meet today. I encourage your HR team to create informal coffee or quarterly afternoon meetings for dyslexic employees to share tips and strategies.

These informal meetings provide the group with an opportunity to discuss problem areas and then develop strategies as a group. Often many of the strategies created by these groups can benefit all employees. The group can also serve as an idea generation group to develop innovative concepts for the company. Dyslexics need to walk and move around while working and thinking. If possible, encourage walk breaks at lunch or at 3:00 pm to break up the day. Tech companies understand the importance of movement and offer activities to encourage walking meetings or releasing energy throughout the day. Suggest to your boss or team members walking half of the meeting. Even taking five or ten minutes to get up and move around can provide a benefit.

Assigned Mentors

When possible, assign dyslexic new hires with a fellow dyslexic employee who has worked for the company for more than three years. During these three years, the individual will have established an informal network and have a solid understanding of the company and its social and political structures. I also recommend pairing the dyslexic mentor with a seasoned non-dyslexic mentor. When John Levell and I talked two years ago, he discussed how his mentor always supported him and how important that was to him.

Management Training

Dyslexia training either in person or via webinars must be included in new hire orientation and ongoing educational training. My son's school district requires all teachers and school staff to attend an extensive three-phase dyslexia training. A two-hour training can provide significant benefits from increased productivity to understanding how dyslexics can provide an advantage. Advanced technologies are changing the future of work and companies will need a multi-diverse talent pool.

The Dyslexia Checklist

The Dyslexia Checklist was inspired from a conversation I had with a dyslexic employee who wished there was a universal checklist.

- Laptop with access to a variety of software applications for checking spelling and word verification.
  - Grammarly
  - Google Chrome (audio dictate)
  - Dictionary

- Access to software applications from Evernote or Canva.

- Engage voice commands.

- Enable audio read capabilities.

- A quiet separate space to work or pre-assigned seating.

- A locker or flat space for folders.

- Earbuds for music or white noise.

- The ability to print emails and documents.

- Access to a study room with a whiteboard.

- Full access to the office supply closet – Post It Notes, different color Sharpies, pens, journals.

- Access to Benq or similar computer screen.

- The option to take walk breaks when needed.

- The flexibility of demonstrating work using infographic format or slide deck.

- Documents like research papers and articles are converted to digital files for audio read functionality.

- Team buddy who can help explain verbally information, formalities, and decipher literal social comments.

- Infographics for workflows, teams, and information that can be shared more efficiently using graphics.

- Team education about dyslexia from strengths to word retrieval misfires.

- Freedom to discuss strategies developed to improve workplace efficiencies without derogatory feedback from immediate bosses and team members.

  - *All employees* should have this freedom, not just us.

Add your ideas here:

Chapter Eleven

Workplace Strategies

"The path to your dream career is rarely straight
and linear."
Ink & Volt

Dyslexics develop adaptive strategies early in life. Many of us have vivid memories from daycare and elementary school as our brains quickly developed survival workarounds. The majority of the strategies are second nature. My brain instantly produces a solution.

These innate strategies are constantly tweaked to match my work and personal environments. Finding tools that work best with your dyslexic brain and productivity work style is essential. For more information about productivity workstyles, check out Carson Tate's book, *Work Simply*.

As mentioned in previous chapters, during interviews with dyslexic professionals, tech support and workplace accommodations were the two most frequently mentioned employment needs. Managing emails and to-do lists ranked third.

Email Response Templates

Responding to the mountain of emails we receive for work can be overwhelming. To simplify email, I save repetitive copy to a Notes or Word file while working on a project. Generally, these are three or four sentences I will need to copy and paste into personalized emails. Everything I write is checked using Grammarly. For important email drafts, the copy rests overnight. In the morning, I read out loud with fresh eyes.

Creating templates increases my writing efficiency and reduces copy errors and dyslexia's misfires. I have a tendency to leave out small connecting words and the "ed" for past tense verbs. With predictive responses now available individuals can use the standard answer and add a few personal comments.

When I receive emails late in the day, that requires a detailed response, I draft the response, and review in the morning prior to sending. For urgent request from clients, I send an email and ask if they are available to speak by phone.

The majority of the time I can quickly assess in a 10 or 15-minute phone call their inquiry faster than engaging in an email chain. We all reach a level of decision fatigue by 5:00 pm. Carson Tate frequently mentions on LinkedIn the importance of developing a system for managing inbound emails and then how to draft response. Developing email management strategies is important as viewing the long list of messages in your inbox can be visually overwhelming

Managing Meetings and Calendars

Half of the professionals interviewed for this book use paper calendars and planners and the other half rely on digital software applications. For my brain, if the information is not tangible, like a sheet of paper, the information does not exist. When I view the meeting invite in Google Calendar, I often invert the time. When I schedule appointments in different time zones, I draw a clock on my whiteboard, and mark the person's time and when I need to call. I must visually see the information.

On Sunday evenings, I list meetings on the calendar whiteboard in my office. If I am meeting someone for lunch, I write down the time I must leave to avoid being late. Meeting times are written in black, action items in blue, and urgent tasks in red. When I look at the whiteboard, I can immediately find the information I am seeking. I print meetings and event announcements and attach to the office bulletin board.

Managing To-Do Lists

Since college, I have used a basic one subject rule spiral notebook to track my action items. On Sunday, I list projects that need to be completed for the week. Each day, I write four to five tasks that must be finished to move the project along. The notebook is for tasks only. I write strategy initiatives and ideas in a journal. Color artists pencils are used to color code projects and tasks. On the opposite page, I make notes from phone conversations. Nothing fancy, one or two phrases to jog my memory. The notebooks are a historical recording of my work.

A brief note about technology and software applications. Always test drive new apps in the evenings or during the weekend to make sure the software is compatible and doesn't create more of a hassle than it's worth. Also, when assembling your workplace strategies, be mindful of adding too many apps and services to avoid feeling overwhelmed. I have found, developing a powerful, simplified toolkit with a mix of tech and old school provides the most benefit.

Chapter Twelve

The Unspoken Side of Dyslexia

"Courage is strengthened by use."
Roger Fritz, *Fast Track*

In the fall of 2016, I hit a wall. I was tired of dancing around my dyslexia misfires and thought, "What the hell, I will tell everyone that I am dyslexic, and that my brain is having an off day." I was done hiding the dyslexia. I knew, by taking one small step, having the courage to tell others that I had a dyslexia misfire and then being willing to roll with the person's response or reaction, would be liberating.

Yes, at times, I still feel fear at the back of my mind. Instead, of giving into that fear, I hold steady, knowing with each step of courage, for me, I become stronger for myself and no one else.

These steps of courage can be attributed to Brene Brown who writes and conducts research about vulnerability. Her *Vulnerability* TED Talk is one of the top ten most viewed videos. Of all the blog posts, articles, and chapters I have written, the next three are the most personal. I share with you the unspoken, darker side of dyslexia. Instead of continuing to cover up or hide, let's find ways to work with the dyslexic brain's most frustrating behaviors. **A word of caution to dyslexic employees.** Consult with an attorney or employment counselor before informing your boss or employer about your dyslexia. My situation is different as my dyslexia is publically known.

Based on interviews and discussions, I have concluded the four most challenging aspects of dyslexia frequently mentioned are word retrieval failure, decoding, social conversations, and walking into black holes. Rarely are these characteristics of dyslexia discussed in the workplace. Last year, I started including *the unspoken aspects of dyslexia* in conference presentations as I believe this topic is important. All four of these traits are the most visual and often determine how others perceive us.

Word, People, Object Retrieval System

Word retrieval is one of the most frustrating aspects of dyslexia. Half the time I feel so dorky when I say the wrong word. I say hot when I mean cold. Or worse – no word comes to mind at all! Literally, there are no thoughts or words, just a blank mental screen. I tell the person, "My dyslexia is mucking up!" or "That was so not the word I was mentally seeking to retrieve!"

Earlier this year, during a business call, my initial response was not coherent when the woman I called answered "hello." My dyslexic brain, in an effort to save time, collapsed three or four sentences into one. Pausing a moment, I told her my word retrieval system was stuck, and the dyslexia was running rampant. She patiently waited while I mentally regrouped. Not everyone is as understanding nor can I control their responses and comments.

Recalling words, objects, and names on demand is a constant challenge. Every time I speak, I don't know for sure which words will be produced. Some words I have spoken sound similar to a foreign language. In the evenings, when my son and I are mentally tired we sing instead of talk. I have discovered this reduces word retrieval problems and makes communication easier. Brandon sings, "I'm tired of homework. I need to sleep. I need to eat. I'm tired of homework. I'm ready for summer again." Then I will sing back a phrase or two. When I am brainstorming, I walk around the house and sing as I can retrieve words faster than writing. As a conference speaker, I verbally organize the speech before building the slide deck for my presentation. Acknowledging the word retrieval system misfires has eased the self-consciousness and reduced the stress of small talk engagement.

During conversations with fellow dyslexics, we discuss how our word retrieval system fails when we are caught off guard or someone makes a rude comment. If the system fails, incorrect words are spoken which, during intense moments, feels more defeating. At that point, I look like a deer caught at night in headlights. I have yet to develop a fail-safe strategy for word retrieval problems. Instead, I pause, take a breather, regroup, and keep going.

What? Can You Repeat What You Just Said?

I am one of the five percent of dyslexics that cannot decode phonetic sounds. In college, I was tested multiples times to validate the dyslexia diagnoses. The specialists determined my brain is unable to decipher sounds to pronounce words. Every word I spell correctly has been memorized with no corresponding sound in my mind. This past week, I was visiting with a friend. He kept saying two words.

To determine what he was saying, I leaned towards him with my left ear close to his face, as if, my ear could grab the sound. My friend kept repeating the word as I moved closer. Finally, I became so frustrated and asked him to spell the word. *"OMG!"* My brain thought. The word started with a "c" instead of an "s" which created more confusion for my brain. I ask Google how to spell a word dozens of times every day.

There are about 30 or 40 words in the English vocabulary that are impossible for me to pronounce or process. I never use these when I speak. On my desk is a stack of notecards with about the same number of words I never can spell or type correctly. I have no muscle memory and have yet to discover an educational tool or trick to retain these annoying words to memory.

Unfortunately, my strategies are the weakest in this area because this is the most challenging aspect of dyslexia that I encounter daily. Outside of Google and my notecards, I am left to ask people multiple times to repeat themselves, back into the meaning of the word by studying the entire sentence, or flat out asking them to spell the word. I feel like the decoding department of my brain is empty.

Saying Hello / Social Conversations

When I was a teenager, my mother would become frustrated when I forgot to say hello at the beginning of a conversation. Even today, I remind my brain to say hello and ask how the other person is doing. My immediate thoughts generally flow effortlessly out of my brain skipping names and greetings. At times, stopping my brain feels like slamming the breaks. However, I know saying "hello" is essential for building relationships. We tend to fire hose our ideas, especially during a conversation when a person's comment triggers connections in our mind. When this happens, most of the social skills we've been taught are tossed out the window as our brains mentally run with the thought.

Engaging in small talk can present communication and social challenges. To help keep a conversation moving along at work, I have a list of questions that I frequently use. For example, "How was your weekend?" or "How is the project coming along?" When I am tired and need more mental time to reply, I use "tell me more" and "that's interesting." For client meetings, I view LinkedIn or Twitter for potential conversational topics. Thinking of responses can feel taxing at times. Creating a list of questions that can be used during networking events, meeting new clients, and building interpersonal relationships helps reduce conversation stress.

Walking into Black Holes

In Chapter 5, I mentioned research by Dr. Michael Ryan. During his studies, he discovered many dyslexics felt like they were walking into black holes each day as they could not predict their brain's responses. Reading through his research, many of the feelings I have had since grade school made sense.

We never know how our brains will behave when we wake in the mornings. Most of the time, our days go as planned. Other times, nothing seems to be working and I feel like calling it a day. Instead, I have learned to take a break, regroup or work on a different project. Most of the time a change of mental scenery settles my dyslexic brain.

Like Chapter 2, I debated including this information in this book. I wondered if discussing the darker side of dyslexia, where our weaknesses live, would strengthen the unconscious bias some individuals have against dyslexia. I thought about the parents last year, who approached me crying after a presentation because someone had finally mentioned what their child was experiencing. Or the individuals at conferences, who quickly stopped by afterwards to say a quiet thank you.

To change the perception of dyslexia in the workplace, we must be able to discuss our weaknesses. Leaders hire professional coaches to strengthen their weaknesses. Like coaches who help leaders, we can create strategies and workarounds to help manage the more frustrating aspects of dyslexia. These challenges should never stand in our way of success.

Chapter Thirteen

Dyslexia and Relationships

*"Maybe we should just date other dyslexics to
save time explaining ourselves."*
—Dyslexic single guy

This past year has been an interesting journey as I
traveled speaking about how dyslexics would rule
the future. During a Q & A session following a
conference presentation, I mentioned a comment
from a friend who is single and dyslexic. A week
prior to the conference we were discussing the
challenges he was encountering while chatting on
Messenger. As I was leaving the conference,
multiple dyslexics approached to share their
dating and relationship stories.

    To research this topic further, I contacted
friends who were single or divorced and dyslexic
to obtain their perspective and to learn more
about their dating challenges. Within a few
weeks, I received messages from individuals who
had heard about my presentation and offered

their dyslexia dating insights. Two married dyslexic couples, I interviewed, believed dating and marrying fellow dyslexics was the best option as it reduces relationship stress. Whereas articles in academic and psychology journals recommended relationships with a dyslexic and non-dyslexic to provide a balance. For dyslexics, I believe finding a partner who supports you is most important regardless if they are dyslexic or not.

Last year, I attended a business happy hour and met Austin. Our hour-long conversation provided the most insight and was one of the most enlightening conversations I had discussing dating, dyslexia, and neurodiversity.

Austin stated, "I know what I want. Since college, I have been the guy that was different, a bit odd to others. I never dated because of my filters. So, I date women who say yes which I have learned is not the best option either. I don't want to settle. I want to find someone who understands I am inflexible and smart."

Austin was my anchor during a business happy hour event. Within minutes of walking into the bar, I met Austin. He is a software entrepreneur. Our conversation evolved to discuss the connection between business ownership and dyslexia.

He said, "Not surprised, really. I have Asperger's. The connection makes sense to me. It's the whole neurodiversity component. Social interactions are difficult, but I force myself to get out and be social." With scientific precision, he described in detail how we have subconsciously developed strategies to appear normal in public with surreal accuracy. Then silence as we digested his assessment.

To this day, I never met anyone who succinctly described our social experiences and how we develop survival strategies similar to the ones we use in business. I believe to our brains, which take information literally, the difference between dating and developing a marketing strategy seems oddly the same.

I found talking to him easier than talking to a non-dyslexic. Not once during the conversation did I have to explain something I said or clean up a dyslexia misfire. Finally, stress-free communication as our conversation moved through a range of topics. We laughed and commented about how we had both successfully navigated an hour of social gymnastics.

Our conversation lingers in my mind. I think about our filters and drive to find someone who will understand and connect with us. Like Austin, I know what I want and don't want. Our need for mental engagement and a constant drive to create and solve complex problems is biological. It's not a switch that can be turned on and off at will. The mental boredom we experience is real. It's physical and requires strategies for accomplishing tasks while honoring the benefits of the dyslexic brain.

Listening to Austin describe how he manages social interactions and the challenges he encounters while dating is similar to comments I hear from single dyslexics. He was recently divorced and had resumed dating again. Before talking to Austin, I had similar discussions with parents who had dyslexic children, and one of the spouses was not dyslexic.

Every individual mentioned the marriage was tested because the non-dyslexic parent felt overwhelmed and out of place. Each family was in search of solutions or strategies to improve the relationships and family dynamics.

The difficult part is describing to others how our brain works and how it impacts our behavior in a way they can understand. One of my male friends mentioned that his former wife always corrected the conversation details when he became confused with the sentence sequencing. After a while, he stopped talking to her and is now divorced.

After dozens of conversations, patterns and trends began to immerge, similar to what I observed while conducting research for *Dyslexia's Competitive Edge*. The feedback from the interviews revealed the challenges encountered while dating is consistent for both men and women. These challenges included boredom, the lack of connection, and mentally leaving the conversation, along with the constant need to explain the social misreads and language misfires. While dating, I have had similar experiences. We can appear to be elusive as we mentally wander off during conversations.

I have spoken with couples who are making the relationship work. "It's not to say we don't have our ups and downs" as one mother said while we chatted. "I'm thankful for my husband. We still have intense fights; however, I know he's committed and makes an effort to understand our son. What I value most about my husband is his willingness to make an effort each time."

Several themes emerged while writing this chapter. Before now, I never considered the kinetic aspect of dyslexia. The physical and biological need to interact with people is important. One of my dyslexic male friends described, during one of our phone chats, how we need to get a kinetic read. He said, "We need to have a physical connection with people. You can't tell from an app and texting. I can't feel if it is a match or not. The kinetic energy is huge for us. I have got to have a gut read on the person to know. With an app, there is nothing."

Another area that creates social and communication problems is that the dyslexic brain tends to interpret comments literally. I have spent, what seems like hours, decoding emojis or Messenger stickers. In a texting environment, we have limited access to non-verbal cues which impedes our ability to read the person and situation. Like single dyslexics I interviewed, I can become lost in the sentence sequencing when texting with non-dyslexics. I am forever scrolling back to the top of the messages to determine what to text next. One dyslexic entrepreneur suggested starting a dating service exclusive for dyslexics. Several dyslexics believed marring dyslexics works best. When starting a new dating relationship, our social behaviors and communication style can present problems, especially when there is a misunderstanding or literal interpretation of the conversation.

An interesting parallel, I noted from my research, is that dyslexics are intuitive and skilled at reading people. The majority of our decisions are made based on our gut intuition. Our perceptions of others are very accurate. However, at the same time, our brains find jokes and literal comments confusing.

Dyslexia is like an onion and marriage at the same time. With each passing year, more information is discovered as we peel away the layers. We gain an understanding and appreciation for the brilliance offered by the dyslexic brain while learning how to be compassionate towards and forgiving of its misfires.

Chapter Fourteen

Dyslexia is a Lifestyle

"To dream by night is to escape your life. To dream by day is to make it happen."
—Stephen Richards

Last fall, I met Ben West at the 2017 International Dyslexia Association Conference. During a break, we talked about our dyslexia habits and behaviors. I said, "Dyslexia is a lifestyle." A fellow dyslexic joined the conversation and agreed. She and her husband were both dyslexic and talked about how they were always managing multiple projects or businesses simultaneously.

Dyslexia is a lifestyle that influences our social interactions, relationships, and careers. Every dyslexic I know looks up when they are thinking of a response. My neighbors often comment that my son and I will wear out the garage door because we are constantly on the move. We're always starting projects, changing things or launching businesses.

Two years ago, I had an idea to remove the front flower bed and started the project at night using the car's headlights to illuminate the yard. At times, I feel driven to feed the hungry dyslexic brain either with new information or to find a challenging problem to solve. Other times, I must get a kinetic fix either by running, dancing or driving go-karts with my son.

From my conversations with fellow dyslexics, I have compiled a list of common behaviors and characteristics. The discussion pool includes over 100 individuals with diverse backgrounds, educational experiences, ages from 10 to 75 years old, representing multiple cultures and countries.

- We all listen to songs or album dozens if not hundreds of times over and over as if our brain is searching for something.

  - As one woman stated at the 2018 SXSWedu Conference, "Once I have consumed the music I'm done. I can't listen to any part of the album again." She said her listening times were in the thousands.

- A common relaxation activity is driving around neighborhoods by yourself or with the dyslexic family members visually redesigning houses or yards. We notice the little things out of place. Redesigning properties or spaces is our favorite mental chew toy.

- During creative flow, we often wear the same clothes and eat the same food. Our focus is singular as we work to complete our creative endeavor which can include businesses, inventions, software applications, movies, books, songs, buildings, and scientific research.

- We feel driven by an invisible force that is almost impossible to describe to others.

- Our physical energy operates in two speeds, we are either moving like a Bugatti or we're asleep. When we must travel in the slow lane, metaphorically speaking, it's difficult to manage the lower gears. Engaging in small talk conversations is an example of operating in the slow lane.

- For adults, about half are divorced. The reasons mentioned were related to communication and lifestyle habits.

- We take comments literally and jokes can throw us off.

- To date, I have yet to find a dyslexic who enjoys small talk. Small talk feels laborious. We prefer to solve complex problems or discuss ideas.

- We are very kinetic individuals which means, we must move to think. For single dyslexics, we need to interact with individuals first to determine if we like them or not before going out on a date.

- When we need a sensory fix; we are either frustrated or experiencing creative energy blockage. Many dyslexics mentioned listening to rock music or rap. Metallica was mentioned frequently as a favorite band.

- Shopping malls are visually overwhelming.

- We visually organize physical spaces or problems.

- We tend to fire hose our ideas when talking with peers. Our brains think greetings such as saying hello are non-essential.

- When our creative problem-solving brain is running full speed, smaller words are deleted when talking. Sometimes we combine two sentences into one to talk faster!

- Remembering people's name is difficult. We can remember details of the conversation from our visual memory.

- We can remember complex information or large bits of data. Yet we have difficulty remembering how to spell our children's names or simple words, like *when* and *fuel*.

- Most of us have at least one whiteboard in our office or at home.

- We think, if we cannot see it, whatever it is, we will forget.

- We know exactly where every piece of paper or statement is on our desk, regardless of the outward appearance.

- We rely on our gut for all our decisions and are highly intuitive individuals.

- We invert words, saying hot when we mean cold or purchase the wrong salad dressing because we misread the label.

- Ambiverts – a high percentage mentioned a hybrid between being an introvert and an extrovert. Several of the dyslexic entrepreneurs I know stated when discussing their ideas, they could talk for hours, however, on a social level they were introverts.

Dyslexia impacts each person in varying degrees, and like an individual's personality, there are no two dyslexics alike. I am always amazed when talking to someone new, how, so many of our behaviors and strengths are similar. We're like an extended family with branches that reach around the world.

Understanding how dyslexia is a lifestyle is important. All of the common characteristics that I listed are part of who we are as individuals. As dyslexia gains awareness within the workplace, hopefully, the need to explain our behaviors will decrease.

Conclusion

"Creativity is the ability to see problems in new ways. Creativity is the ability to see things in new light or from a different perspective. Creativity is the knack of looking for answers in unexpected places."
—Betty Ewards, *Drawing on the Artist Within*

I am not my dyslexia nor am I defined by its limitations. Instead, I am an author who writes thought-provoking books about topics I believe are important.

Because I write and speak about dyslexia, most individuals instantly think I work in education or am a parent advocate. Which highlights, the problem, the perception of dyslexia continues to be viewed as an educational topic that is addressed during school.

When I titled this book, *How Dyslexics Will Rule the Future*, I had a mission, to sell enough copies to gain a top 20 ranking on the *New York Times* best-selling list. I imagined how good it would feel to say "Yes!" knowing the title would send a message to the world. Having *How*

Dyslexics Will Rule the Future ranked in a best-selling position would move dyslexia into the mainstream and be recognized with other important non-fiction topics.

This book's title would serve as invitation to individuals to learn more about dyslexia and how the benefits of thinking differently can be applied in the workplace. The subtitle reminds readers of the importance of creative, problem-solvers.

In November of 2015, I started studying and researching how AI and automation would impact employment and our economy. The initial research evolved into this book. Articles discussing AI, automation, the future of work, and dyslexia were intermittent until recently.

In the past nine months, I have noticed a significant increase in articles about these topics. New dyslexia groups have formed around the world to generate awareness and to help individuals find employment that matches their strengths and dyslexia talents. In the U.K and parts of northern Europe, new organizations and companies have formed to provide employment and workplace assistance to dyslexic adults. Exceptional Individuals and Future of ND are two new groups helping dyslexic professionals in the workplace.

Progress is being made in developing countries from Africa to parts of India and Southeast Asia. I receive emails from individuals from countries all around the world seeking advice or sharing information about new schools and dyslexia initiatives. Dyslexic individuals in every corner of the world are working to make a difference.

Similar to a TEDx Talk, I will close this book with a call to action. After completing this book, I believe human creativity and ingenuity is more important now than ever before and is one of the most powerful talents we possess. Our ability to develop a new idea or concept separates us from the rest of the animal kingdom and advanced machines we have built. With the rapid advancement of technology, I believe our hyper focus on STEM is decreasing the importance of creativity. We must recognize the importance of human creativity and how it is the foundation for *everything* from problem-solving to developing new ideas.

I was surprised by how protective I've become of my creativity. Social media scrolling is no longer appealing as I carve time in my schedule to write offline in journals while sitting outside. I am changing my behaviors to protect my innate thoughts.

My call to action for you, the reader is the following. If you are dyslexic – protect and cultivate your creativity.

HR professionals – develop initiatives to make significant long-term changes at your employer where neurodiversity is welcomed and viewed as a benefit for all.

Educators and parents – teach individuals about dyslexia. Educate from a broader lens to include our strengths and how our visual intellect and creative, problem-solving skills have real, tangible value in the workplace. Most important to all, remember dyslexia and neurodiversity is a lifestyle that doesn't disappear with we graduate high school.

Dyslexics are visionaries. We are the creatives of humanity. Our DNA coding remains for reasons unknown to us. To fully utilize the brilliance of the dyslexic brain now and in the future, we must change the perception of dyslexia in the workplace and develop programs that emphases the three most valuable skills needed for the Fourth Phase of the Industrial Revolution, creativity, problem-solving, and critical thinking. The dyslexic brain was genetically coded to understand, design, and provide an ethical balance in our new digital tech visual intelligence-based world.

Dyslexia U.S. Resources

Dyslexic Advantage

A U.S. based non-profit that focuses on providing positive information about the advantages of dyslexia. The organization provides resources, videos, and articles.
https://www.dyslexicadvantage.org/

International Dyslexia Association

The organization focuses on education and increasing the awareness of dyslexia.
https://dyslexiaida.org/

Inventive Labs

To provide support to dyslexic entrepreneurs.
https://www.inventivelabs.org

Different Brains

A non-profit focused on providing education and
resources for all neurodiverse individuals.
https://www.differentbrains.org

Understood

A non-profit educational based organization that provides information and resources for dyslexics and individuals with learning difference.
https://www.understood.org/en

Elisheva Schwartz

Dyslexia podcast and interviews. For daily quotes and inspiration follow the Dyslexia Quest on Instagram. In August 2017, I was interviewed by Schwartz.
http://www.elishevaschwartz.com/

My interview With Schwartz

http://www.elishevaschwartz.com/podcast/dyslexia-20-the-gift-of-innovation-and-entrepreneurial-mind-with-tiffany-sunday/

Grammarly

In every presentation and book, I have mentioned Grammarly. It is my number one go to tool for writing.
www.grammarly.com

Global Dyslexia Resources

ACM SIGGRAH

An international professional organization of individuals who have an interest or work with computer graphics and design interactive visual images. Members include artists, developers, filmmakers, scientists and business professionals.
https://www.siggraph.org/

The Adult Dyslexia Organization

The organization provides workplace support and resources for adults with dyslexia.
https://www.dyslexia.uk.net/adults-with-dyslexia/

British Dyslexia Association
U.K. based organization focuses on education and increasing the awareness of dyslexia.
https://www.bdadyslexia.org.uk/

Center for Child Evaluation and Teaching (Kuwait)
www.ccerkuwait.org

The Codpast

Sean Douglas has built an amazing resource for individuals with dyslexia. He posts video blogs, how-to videos, and information to help the global dyslexia community. https://thecodpast.org/

Dyslexia Association of Ireland
www.dyslexia.ie

Dyslexia Scotland
https://www.dyslexiascotland.org.uk

Dyslexia Association of Singapore
www.das.org.sg/

Dyslexia Nigeria
http://www.dyslexianigeria.com

Exceptional Individuals

Employment recruiting agency for dyslexic professionals in the U.K.
https://www.exceptionalindividuals.com

Evolution in Leadership

Company that helps dyslexic entrepreneurs overcome their challenges.
https://www.evolutioninleadership.com

Half Penny Development Ltd.
http://wwwhalfpennydevelopment.co.uk
Lexxic

A U.K. based organization that provides support and resources for adults with dyslexia and learning differences. http://www.lexxic.com

Made by Dyslexia

A new non-profit organization based in London, England and is supported by Richard Branson. http://madebydyslexia.org

Maharashtra Dyslexia Association (India)
www.mdamumbai.com

U.K. Academy
https://www.vercida.com/uk

Veercida

Employment search to help everyone find a job, based in the U.K.
https://www.vercida.com/uk

Recommended Books

The Gifts of Imperfection by Brene Brown

The Second Machine Age by Erik Brynjolfsson and Andrew McAfee

9 Things You Simply Must Do by Dr. Henry Cloud (one of my favorite books)

Necessary Endings by Dr. Henry Cloud (another favorite)

A Whole New Mind by Dan Pink

Free Agent Nation: The Future of Working for Yourself by Dan Pink

Work Simply by Carson Tate (great book for work)

Seeing What Others Cannot See by Thomas G. West

In the Mind's Eye by Thomas G. West

In Our Own Image by George Zarkadakis

TEDx Talks and Videos

Brene Brown – TEDx
The Power of Vulnerability
https://youtu.be/iCvmsMzlF7o

The Codpast YouTube Channel
https://www.youtube.com/user/thecodpast

Kate Griggs – TEDx
The Creative Brilliance of Dyslexia
https://youtu.be/CYM40HN82l4

Sir Ken Robinson – TEDx
How Schools Kill Creativity
https://youtu.be/iG9CE55wbtY

Tiffany Sunday – TEDx
Dyslexia 2.0: The Gift of Innovation and Entrepreneurial Mind
https://youtu.be/kAGyHpggMQY

Bibliography

Austin, R.D., Pisano, G.P., "Neurodiversity as a Competitive Advantage". *Harvard Business Review*. May – June 2017.

Abraham, Magid and Marco Annuziata. "Augmented Reality Is Already Improving Worker Performance" *Harvard Business Review*. March 13, 2017.

Bishop, Peter C. and Andy Hines, *Teaching the Future* Palgrave Macmillan. London. 2012.

Brynjoleffon, Erik and Andrew McAfee. *The Second Machine Age* New York: W.W. Norton & Company, 2014.

Carr, Nicholas. *The Glass Cage* New York: W.W. Norton & Company, 2014.

Clegg, Alicia, "Dyslexia, Dyspraxia, Dyscalculia: the Gains for Employers" *Financial Times* January 15, 2018.

Deloitte Consulting. *2017 Deloitte Global Human Capital Reports* New York, 2017.

Duncan, Ross. "Don't waste our superpowers: let's help managers support neurodiverse civil servants" *Civil Service World* July 30, 2018.

Di Fiore, Alessandro "A Chief Innovation Officer's Actual Responsibilities" *Harvard Business Review*. November 26, 2014.

Div, Lior. "How my dyslexia launched my hacking career" *CSO* January 27, 2016.

Edathikunnel, Tom. "AI is redefining the meaning of 'human' in human resources" *The Ladders* February 4, 2018.

EY Press Release. "EY is #1 for Diversity & Inclusion, according to *DiversityInc* Top 50 Companies for Diversity List" May 2017.

Fritz, Roger. *Fast Track How to Gain and Keep Momentum* Naperville: Inside Advantage, 1999.

Friedman, Thomas. "While You Were Sleeping" *New York Times*. January 16, 2018.

Godin, Seth. *The Icarus Deception* London: Penguin, 2012.

HR Daily Advisor "Hiring in 2018: Why Neurodiversity Matters" January 22, 2018.

Heater, Brian. "Technology is killing jobs, and only technology can save them" *Tech Crunch* March 26, 2017.

Hewlett, Sylvia Ann. "Millennials with Disabilities: A Large, Invisble Talent Cohort with Innovative Potential" *Inc.* February 12, 2018.

Jacobs, Brian. "Launching Neurodiversity at Your Company – Get the Benefits of Differently-abled Employees in Your Workplace. *Encap* July 31, 2017.

Kaufman, Scott Barry. "The Real Neuroscience of Creativity" *Scientific America* August 19, 2013.

Kearns, Michael. "The of End of Traditional Employment – The Other Gig Economy" *Topal* December 18, 2017.

Kehe, Jason. "Swarming Trend: A Plague of Hyperbole" *Wired Magazine* August 2018.

Lewis, Katherine. "The New Frontier in Workplace Diversity: Brain Differences" *Fortune* December 16, 2014.

Logan, Julie. "Analysis of the Incidence of Dyslexia in Entrepreneurs and Its Implications" *USASBE* 2008 Proceeding.

Lubell, Sam. "Will algorithms be the new architect?" *Dwell* July/August 2018.

Marr, Bernard. "The Key Definitions of Artificial Intelligence (AI) That Explains Its Importance" *Forbes* February 14, 2018.

Morrow, Monique. "Trends of 2018: What the New Year Brings for Technology and The World Around Us" *LinkedIn* December 7, 2017.

Nerenberg, Jenara. "Innovation in your inbox" *Fast Company* January 15, 2018.

Palermo, Elizabeth. "Who Invented the Printing Press?" *Life Science*. February 25, 2014.

Patterson, Gavin. "Neurodiversity is an asset in the digital age" *World Economic Forum* January 19, 2018.

Philipson, Alice. "GCHG employs more than 100 dyslexic and dyspraxic spys" *Telegraph* September 21, 2014.

Pierce, David. "Enjoy Your New Virtual Office" *Wired Magazine* February 2018.

Pistrui, Joseph. "The Future of Work is Imagination, Creativity, and Strategy" *Harvard Business Review* January 18, 2018.

Rander, Michael. "Digitalist: The Rise of the Digital Workforce" *SAP* May 9, 2016.

Rogers, Charlotte. "The Brand Benefits of Neurodiversity" *Marketing Week* May 31, 2017.

Ryan, Michael, M.D. "Social and Emotional Problems Related to Dyslexia" *International Dyslexia Association* December 18, 2017.

Manyika, James. "What is the future of work?" *McKinsey Global Institute* December 2017.

Schneps, Matthew. "The Advantages of Dyslexia" *Scientific American* August 19, 2014.

Schneps, Matthew. "Dyslexia Can Deliver Benefits" *Scientific American* December 18, 2014.

Shamdasan, Jasia. "New centre for dyslexic people will use VR tech to enhance learning" *The New Paper* June 1, 2018.

Visual Spatial Organization "Spatial Strenghts" www.visualspatial.com June 27, 2018.

Selingo, Jeff. "Here's what will happen when millions of jobs are lost to robots" *CNBC* December 30, 2016.

Steward, Heather. "Robot revolution: rise of 'thinking machines' could exacerbate inequity" *Guardian* January 1, 2018.

Talent Smart. "9 Signs That You're An Ambivert" February 26, 2018.

Tate, Carson. *Work Simply* Peguin Group. New York, 2015.

Trunk, Penelope. *Brazen Careerist: The New Rules for Success* New York: Hachette Book, 2007.

Warren, Tom. "Microsoft Word now reads text aloud to help people with dyslexia" *The Verge* August 1, 2017.

Wallace, Kelly. "The genius in people with learning disabilities, mental health disorders" *CNN*, March 9, 2017.

West, Tomas G. *Seeing What Others Cannot See* New York: Prometheus Books, 2017.

West, Thomas G. *In the Mind's Eye* New York: Prometheus Books, 2009.

World Economic Forum, Future of Jobs Report. 2016.

Zarkadakis, George. "Artificial Intelligence in the Workplace: Replacing Jobs – Myth or Fact? *GOARYA* March 14, 2018.

Zarkadakis, George. "Forget algorithms. The future of AI is hardware!" *Huffington Post* January 15, 2018.

Zarkadakis, George. *In Our Own Image* New York: Pegasus Books, 2015.

Acknowledgments

This book represents hundreds of conversations with professionals with dyslexia, scholars, researchers, entrepreneurs, non-dyslexics, and parents or spouses of dyslexics. This book is different from my previous two, as I pushed the envelope to drive change. A new model must be created to make the old model obsolete.

During the past two years, *How Dyslexics Will Rule the Future* would not have been possible without the following individuals.

My editor, Mary Lewis who carefully worked through the manuscript.

This book would not have been possible without the constant support from my son, Brandon Belanger. He provided recommendations and helped around the house so that I could write and rewrite and the chapters.

To my close circle of friends who provide support – Brad Bush, Blake Brownlee, Skip Howard, and Kevin Koym. To the dyslexia community, Thomas West, Ben West, Rob Austin, Chontae Feldman, Debbie Ripchick, and Laura Dyslexic Jackson-Cavalleri. To fellow authors who offered their support, Payne Harrison and George Zarkadakis.

Most importantly all my readers and TEDx supporters who share their inspiring stories. I am humbled and thankful to be part of an amazing global community.

About the Author

Tiffany Sunday is the author of *Dyslexia's Competitive Edge* and *You Posted What!?*. Tiffany is internationally known for her books and TEDx Talk *Dyslexia 2.0: The Gift of Innovation and Entrepreneurial Mind*. She presents at conferences in the U.S. and U.K and has been interviewed by WFAA-ABC, BBC, CNN Radio, and quoted in *Forbes, USA Today, The Dallas Morning News, The Austin-American Statesman, The Dallas Business Journal, Restaurant News*, and more. She lives in Dallas, Texas with her son, Brandon.

Made in the USA
Columbia, SC
05 November 2018